REDNECK
DICTIONARY
III

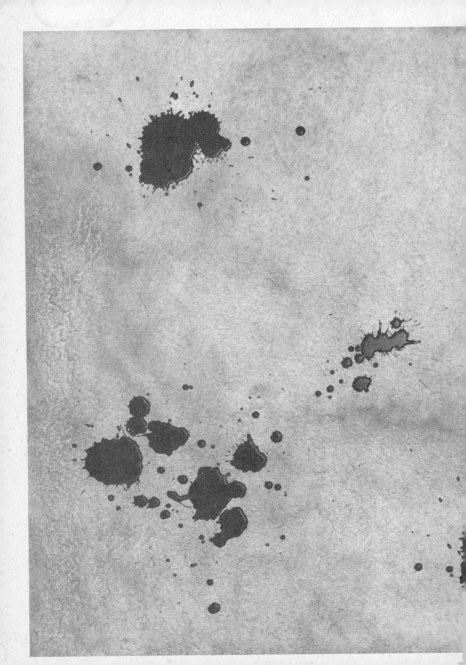

REDNECK DICTIONARY

III

*Learning to Talk
More Gooder Fastly*

Jeff Foxworthy

with Fax Bahr, Adam Small,
Garry Campbell, and Brian Hartt

Illustrations by Layron DeJarnette

VILLARD NEW YORK

Published in the United States by Villard Books, an imprint of The Random House Publishing Group, a division of Random House, Inc., New York.

VILLARD and "V" CIRCLED Design are registered trademarks of Random House, Inc.

Library of Congress Cataloging-in-Publication Data
Foxworthy, Jeff.
Jeff Foxworthy's redneck dictionary III: learning to talk more gooder fastly / Jeff Foxworthy, with Fax Bahr . . . [et al.];
illustrations by Layron DeJarnette.
p.   cm.
ISBN 978-0-345-49848-9
1. Rednecks—Humor.   2. Vocabulary—Humor.   3. English language—Southern States—Humor.   I. Bahr, Fax.   II. Title.
III. Title: Jeff Foxworthy's redneck dictionary 3.
IV. Title: Jeff Foxworthy's redneck dictionary three.
V. Redneck dictionary III.
PN6231.R38F6743   2007
818'.5402—dc22   2007027535

Printed in the United States of America on acid-free paper

www.villard.com

246897531

First Edition

Book design by Susan Turner

REDNECK
DICTIONARY
III

ACNE

Aa

abil·i·ties (ə-bil´-ət-ēz), *n. and pron.* a statement of charges for services rendered and subsequent action to be taken by a specified male person. *"I don't care if he's broke, Ma, the house payment's **abilities** got to pay."*

ac·ne (ak´-nē), *v. and n.* concerning a male person's behavior and the result of that behavior. *"Once again we took him to a fancy restaurant, and he didn't know how to **acne** made a fool of himself."*

ac·quire (ə-kwīər´), *n.* a group of singers, especially those who perform during religious ceremonies. *"She sings so pretty, she should join **acquire**."*

ac·quit (ə-kwit´), *n. and v.* a personal declaration of resignation from an assigned task. *"You ain't firin' me, 'cuz **acquit**!"*

ac·tiv·ist (akt´-əv-ist), *v. and conj.* to behave in a certain manner, particularly one based on another reality. *"She seduced me into signing that petition, and now she activist she don't know me!"*

ad·min·is·ter (at-mi´-nə-stər), *adj. and n.* a specific clergyman or agent of a government, as designated by the observer. *"I tell ya, administer is a good man."*

af·ford (ə-fȯrd´), *n.* an automobile manufactured by the motor company that produced the Model T. *"If I had the money for a car, I'd want to buy afford."*

air·line (er´-līn), *adv. and v.* concerning the location and dishonesty of the person being addressed or discussed. *"Don't sit airline about it, boy . . . tell the truth!"*

AIRLINE

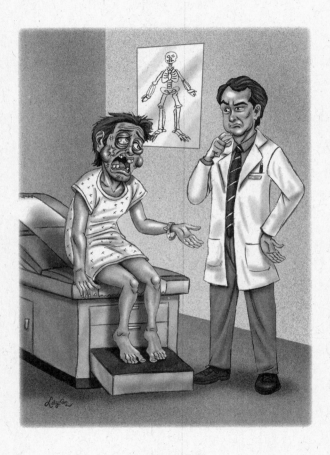

ANARCHIST

al·i·bi (al´-ə-bī), *n. and v.* the predicted future purchases by a male named Albert, Alfred, or Alvin. *"We always invite Al, 'cause **alibi** drinks for everybody."*

anal (ān´-ȯl), *v. and pron.* being inferior to what one expects. *"Enemas **anal** they're cracked up to be."*

an·ar·chist (an-ər-kist´), *conj., n., and v.* additionally, having pressed one's lips to another's as an expression of affection or sensual desire. *"**Anarchist** her ma, **anarchist** her sister, **anarchist** her gramma, **anarchist** her other sister, **anarchist** her other other sister, and then her dad walked in and . . ."*

an·noys (ə-nȯiz´), *n.* a loud or irritating sound. *"Well, I wouldn't've peed my pants if I hadn't heard **annoys**!"*

ant·hill (ən-til´), *conj.* up to a point in time. *"I won't set foot in that room **anthill** he cleans it up!"*

an·ti·pas·to (an´-tē-past-ə), *n. and v.* to discharge from the body, as done by the female sibling of a parent of the speaker. *"After eatin' all that salami last night, my **antipasto** kidney stone."*

ar·chery (ärch´-ər-ē), *n. and conj.* a male person's ultimatum relating to a curved structure, usually one that serves as the roof or overhang of a passageway. *"He went off to St. Louis, sayin' he was dang sure he was goin' to see the **archery** weren't coming back."*

Ar·i·zo·na (er´-əz-ōn-ə), *n., v., and adv.* phrase delimiting the quality of the gaseous atmosphere surrounding the earth. *"I'd move to Denver, but with all the smog that **Arizona** slightly better than it is here in L.A."*

ANTHILL

ATMOSPHERE

Ar·kan·sas (ärk´-ən-sȯ), *n. and v.* a flat-bottomed boat in conjunction with an observer's visual perception. *"Noah finished the **Arkansas** that it was good."*

ar·son (ar´-sən), *adj. and n.* pertaining to the male offspring of the speaker. *"I know I swore **arson** didn't set fire to your car, Sheriff, but I guess I misspoke."*

at·mo·sphere (ət´-məs-fir), *pron. and v.* a conjecture about the feelings of anxiety of a certain being. *"The way that ol' Red tucks his tail, now, that's a dog **atmosphere** his owner."*

at·trac·tor (ə-trak´-tər), *n.* a motor-propelled machine used mainly in agriculture. *"My uncle cuts his grass with **attractor**."*

Au·di (aú´-dē), *n.* a protrusion; usually used to describe the knotted flesh on the stomach of a human left after the severing of the umbilical cord. *"Most people have an 'innie,' but Roy's belly button is definitely an **Audi**."*

au·ra (ȯr´-ə), *conj. and adj.* a phrase indicating a choice between one thing and another. *"You gettin' a Quarter Pounder **aura** Big Mac?"*

au·to·mate (ȯ´-tə-māt), *v.* a suggestion for procreation. *"I know we just met tonight, baby, but I think we **automate**."*

 Bb

bar·i·um (ber´-ē-əm), *v. and n.* to deposit a male person or animal underground and cover him with earth. *"My dog died yesterday, so we're gonna **barium** today."*

AUTOMATE

BATTERY

bar·rel (ber´-əl), *n. and v.* a large, thick-furred, om-
nivorous mammal of the family Ursidae and its predicted actions. *"A wolverine'll mess you up, but a **barrel**
kill you."*

bat·tery (ba´-tər-ē), *n. and pron.* a baseball player
who regularly attempts an offensive maneuver
wherein he uses a club to strike a ball thrown in his
direction. *"Stan ain't half the **battery** used to be."*

be·hav·ior (bi-hāv´-yər), *v. and adj.* a phrase connecting the manner in which a person conducts him-
or herself to someone or something possessed by or
related to that person. *"If you don't **behavior** daddy's
gonna spank you!"*

Bei·rut (bā´-rüt), *adj. and n.* a path that crosses or
follows the contours of a broad inlet of water that
curves into a landmass. *"I guess old Doug decided to
take the **Beirut**."*

be·nign (bē-nīn´), *v. and adj.* to reach a level of one increment more than eight. *"The scar from your tumor removal is going to **benign** inches long."*

bor·der (bȯr´d-ər), *v. and n.* to have made a female feel uninterested and fatigued, as through tedious action or talk. *"She said she left him because he **border** to death."*

bor·row (bär´-ō), *n. and v.* a phrase concerning the future state of a tavern. *"Hurry up or the **borrow** be closed!"*

bot·tle (bät´-əl), *n. and v.* the corporeal form of a being and its future state. *"If you keep eatin' and drinkin' like that, your **bottle** go bad."*

BOTTLE

BULLETIN

boy·sen·berry (bȯiz-ən-ber´-ē), *n., conj., and v.* a phrase connecting a group of males to the act of interring a being or thing underground. *"Get this guy before the cops show up."*

brid·al (brīd´-əl), *n. and v.* a betrothed female and her future state. *"If the preacher don't move it along, the **bridal** have her baby right there on the altar."*

bu·lim·ia (bə-lē´-mē-ə) *v. and n.* a demand that one accept the speaker's truthfulness. *"**Bulimia** don't want to eat that again."*

bul·le·tin (bu´-lət-in), *n. and prep.* a metal projectile intended for use in a firearm and its position with relation to the interior of an object. *"If you want to save us, you're gonna have to put a **bulletin** that gun."*

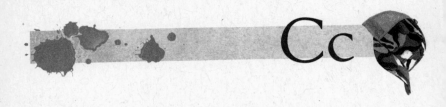

ca·chet (ka-shāʹ), *n. and pron.* currency, in relation to a group of people. *"He spent every cent of the **cachet** gave him before he got kicked out of that casino."*

ca·dav·er (kəd-avʹ-ər), *v. and adj.* pertaining to the possibility of gaining possession of something belonging to a female. *"The coroner had to get back to the morgue, but she said I **cadaver** fries."*

ca·jole (kə-jōlʹ), *v. and n.* a request for action from a group. *"I don't like being the center of attention, so **cajole** stop staring at me?"*

Ca·jun (kājʹ-ən), *n. and conj.* an enclosed space used to confine a being, especially as connected with an action. *"They just threw that bear in a **Cajun** left him there."*

CAJOLE

CAPABLE

can·ni·bal (kan´-ə-búl), *v. and n.* interrogative concerning the abilities of an uncastrated male bovine. *"I've always wondered, **cannibal** mate with more than one cow in a day?"*

can·ter (kan´-tər), *v. and adj.* negative interrogative concerning the abilities of someone connected to a female. *"**Canter** sister watch the baby?"*

can·ti·na (kan-tē´-nəh), *v. and n.* interrogative concerning the actions or abilities of a person who uses a nickname for Christine. *"Hey, **cantina** bring us a couple of cold beers?"*

ca·pa·ble (kāp´-ə-búl), *n., adj., and n.* a garment that ties at the neck and hangs across the back and its association with an uncastrated male bovine. *"Soon as he sees a red **capable** will attack."*

car·cass (kär´-kəs), *n. and conj.* the reason for an action or event related to a motor vehicle. *"My daddy won't let me drive his **carcass** I've hit too many deer."*

car·di·gan (kärd-ə-gin), *n. and adv.* repeated action upon or using a small, rectangular piece of cardboard adorned with rank and suit. *"Something's fishy with this deck, 'cause you just played the same **cardigan**."*

cat·tle (kat´-əl), *n. and v.* a feline creature and its future actions. *"Be careful, that old **cattle** scratch your eyes out if you get anywhere near her."*

cau·li·flow·er (kȯl´-ə-flaů-ər), *v. and n.* to verbally describe the reproductive organs of an angiospermous plant. *"You can't **cauliflower** anything but beautiful."*

CARDIGAN

CERTIFY

cel·lar (sel´-ər), *v. and adj.* to trade a thing in a female's possession for currency. *"My sister is so broke she had to **cellar** entire collection of fine wines."*

cen·ter (sent´-ər), *v. and n.* to urge, instruct, or propel a female into action. *"Soon as she started in with her naggin' I **center** packing."*

cen·ti·me·ter (sent´-ə-mē-tər) *v. and n.* to be ordered or instructed to await the arrival of a female person. *"My gramma's coming in on the train, and I been **centimeter**."*

cer·ti·fy (sər´-təf-ī), *n. and conj.* a phrase applying a condition or assumption to the use of a formal term for a male person. *"I wouldn't've called her **certify** had known it was a woman."*

cin·em·a (sin´-əm-ə), *v. and n.* to cause a thing to be delivered to a male. *"I was so mad at the producer of that movie, I **cinema** letter givin' him a piece of my mind."*

cir·cus (sər´-kəs), *n. and conj.* a formally addressed justification of actions, as spoken to male person. *"I can't refund your money **circus** I don't work here."*

city (sit´-ē), *v. and n.* the act of reclining onto the buttocks, as connected with a male's subsequent response or action. *"On account of his hemorrhoids, every time he tries to **city** screams."*

clar·i·fy (kler´-əf-ī), *adj. and conj.* the dependence of the lucidity of a thing or concept on another condition or action. *"I'm not **clarify** should stay or go."*

CITY

CLOSER

cli·mate (klīm´-ət), *v. and n.* to ascend a thing. *"Soon as I set my eyes on a mountain, I'm not satisfied till I climate."*

clos·er (klōz´-ər), *v. and adj.* to discontinue or shut something of a female's. *"Please tell her to closer mouth when she eats."*

com·i·cal (kä´-mik-əl), *n. and v.* a person whose profession is causing amusement and his or her future actions. *"That comical make you laugh your head off."*

con·sid·er (kən-sid´-ər), *v. and n.* to be capable of placing a female in the position of resting on her buttocks. *"Sure Ma's senile, but I consider down in the park for hours while I go to the casino."*

con·spire (kən-spīr´), *v. aux. and v.* to perceive a female through the ocular organs. *"With them stupid hats she wears, I **conspire** comin' a couple of blocks away."*

con·stab·u·lary (kän-stab´-ū-lar-ē), *n. and v.* the capability of a convicted criminal to use a sharpened object to wound the flesh of a person named Lawrence. *"You can't work at the prison if you keep letting some **constabulary**."*

cop·per (käp´-ər), *n. and conj.* a choice between a law enforcement officer and someone else. *"Any sixth grader with a full beard is either a **copper** a narc."*

coun·ter·feit (kaúnt´-ər-fit), *n. and v.* a flat surface used for storage, the transaction of business, or dining, and its dimensions with respect to those of a specific place. *"We shoulda measured the kitchen first, 'cuz no amount of money'll make this **counterfeit** in there."*

CONSPIRE

CROTCHETY

cou·ple (kəp´-əl), *n. and v.* an eight-ounce container for measuring liquids and its future state. *"If you wanna party with pure grain, one **couple** do the trick."*

crotch·ety (krä´-chət-ē), *n. and pron.* a phrase connecting a male to a place where two things join, as in where the legs meet on the human body. *"I wouldn't be so cranky if it wasn't my **crotchety** hit with a bat."*

Cu·ba (kyü´-bə), *n. and prep.* a three-dimensional square-sided object with relation to the substance that composes it. *"Want me to put a **Cuba** ice in your drink?"*

Dd

dairy (der´-ē), *v. and n.* the audacity or bravery of a male. *"With that cow Ted's married to, how **dairy** say something about my wife."*

Da·mas·cus (dəm´-ask-əs), *n. and v.* involving a question posed by more than one person to more than one person. *"**Damascus** where we was the night Toby's Bar burned down, but we didn't say nothin'."*

deci·bel (des´-ə-bəl), *n. and v.* a declaration that an observed thing is an uncastrated male bovine. *"You ain't getting' any milk from it 'cuz **decibel**."*

de·cide (di-sīd´), *n.* the position to the right or left of the front or back of an object or being. *"We've concluded that he resembles a pear if you look at him from **decide**."*

de·feat (di-fēt´), *n.* the lower extremities, upon which a creature ambulates. *"That's gonna be one big dog, judgin' by the size of **defeat**."*

DEFEAT

DEFENDER

de·fend·er (di-fen´-dər), *n.* a metal guard positioned over the wheel of a motor vehicle. *"The grille's okay, but **defender** is torn up real bad."*

de·fined (di-find´), *n.* an unexpected discovery. *"That old dictionary you got at the yard sale is **defined** of the century."*

de·liv·er (di-li´-vər), *n.* a large, glandular organ in the body that assists in the metabolic process. *"Considering how much our mailman drinks, I don't know how **deliver** on him holds up."*

de·mand·ed (dih-man´-did), *n. and v.* a male person's past actions. *"It ain't right they fired him, 'cuz **demanded** everything they told him to."*

de·sign (di-zīn´), *n.* a poster or board that identifies, advertises, warns, or indicates the purpose of a thing. *"And **design** said long-haired freaky people need not apply."*

de·spair (dis-per´), *adj. and n.* a particular set of two of something. *"**Despair** is the best hand I had all night."*

de·ten·tion (di-ten´-chən), *n.* special notice taken of a person or thing. *"**Detention** he gives that woman just makes you sick."*

di·al (dī´-əl), *v. and n.* a phrase connecting the possible termination of life to the speaker. *"If your fish **dial** be devastated."*

DESIGN

DINETTE

di·late (dī′-lāt), *v. and adv.* to experience the termination of life well into a specified temporal period. *"I hope I **dilate** in life."*

di·lem·ma (də-le′-mə), *prep. and n.* a phrase connecting an action up to a certain point in time with a person named Emma. *"Wait **dilemma** gets home and finds out you broke her favorite TV."*

di·nette (dīn-ət′), *v. and prep.* to eat supper out, with reference to a specific location. *"I don't want to **dinette** this restaurant ever again."*

di·no·saur (dī′-nə-sȯr) *n., v., and pron.* a person named Dinah having visually perceived something belonging or related to her. *"After she invested in the T. rex museum, **dinosaur** life savings go down the drain."*

dis·arm (dis-ärm´), *adj. and n.* a specified unit, support, or appendage; in particular, the human forelimb. *"I'm goin' to the doctor, 'cuz **disarm** is killing me."*

di·sas·ter (di-sas´-tər), *adv. and v.* a phrase used to persuade someone to inquire something of a female person, by characterizing the inquiry as simple and easy. *"She's bound to break my heart, but I **disaster** out anyway."*

dis·count (dis-kaúnt´), *adv. and v.* to instruct another to merely list numbers consecutively. *"You **discount** to a hundred, and we'll hide."*

dis·cussed (dis-kəst´), *adv. and v.* to have recently used profanity. *"I'm probably gonna get kicked out of school 'cuz my mama **discussed** out the principal again."*

DISARM

DISGUISE

dis·guise (dis-gīz´), *adj. and n.* a specified male person and his current actions or state. *"I don't think **disguise** wearing a mask."*

dish·wash·er (dish´-wä-shər), *adv. and v.* a phrase indicating the speaker's desire for a specific female person to merely perform routine ablutions. *"I know the cook doesn't clean her pots, but I wish she'd **dishwasher** hands."*

dis·lo·cat·ed (dis-lō´-kā-təd), *pron. and v.* a thing situated in a specific physical place. *"We need to find the doctor's office **dislocated** on the second floor."*

dis·mem·ber (dis-mem´-bər), *adv. and v.* to recall; often used as a plea or an imperative. *"We could butcher that hog if I could **dismember** where I put my cleaver."*

dis·play (dis-plā´), *adv. and v.* to simply participate in a recreational activity. *"Quit whining and **display** the game!"*

dis·solve (dis-sälv´), *adv. and v.* to achieve a quick resolution to or completion of a problem. *"You got enough clues, **dissolve** the dang puzzle!"*

doc·tor·ate (däk´-tər-ət), *v. and n.* to change or modify something. *"We can make your medical résumé look better if we **doctorate** up a little bit."*

dog·wood (dòg´-wúd), *n. and v.* the past or conditional actions of a canine. *"I'm in this tree 'cuz otherwise that **dogwood** bite me."*

DISSOLVE

DOODLE

dol·lar (däl´-ər), *n. and conj.* an alternative between a toy figure in human form and something else. *"Is that cashier a living **dollar** what?"*

doo·dle (düd´-əl), *n. and v.* a male person and his predicted actions. *"Don't even look at him, 'cuz that **doodle** kill you."*

drib·ble (drib´-əl), *n. and v.* a cut of meat including a curved bone protruding from the spine and its predicted state. *"If you smother it in barbecue sauce, **dribble** taste much better."*

du·ty (dü´-tē), *v. and n.* to act in the same manner as a specified male. *"If the guy got ya, just **duty** did: light a bag of crap on fire and put it on his porch."*

Ee

east·ern (ēsʹ-tərn), *n. and v.* indicating a change in a male. *"He was a cute baby, but **eastern** into a real monster."*

ego (ēʹ-gō), *n. and v.* a male moving from one location to another. *"He's a good man, Daddy . . . **ego** to church every Sunday."*

eighty (āʹ-tē), *v. and n.* a male, after mastication. *"Right after the old guy **eighty** blew chunks in my car."*

Ei·sen·how·er (īʹ-zən-haủ-ər), *n. and v.* a personal declaration concerning an action or condition lasting for one twenty-fourth of the earth's revolution on its axis. *"Last time Mamie spent the night, **Eisenhower** late for work."*

EASTERN

ELEGANCE

el·der (el´-dər), *v. and n.* to embrace or restrain a female. *"After the old lady mugged us, Junior **elder** down
till the cops arrived."*

el·e·gance (el´-i-gəns), *adj. and prep.* a group either in opposition or in close physical proximity.
*"They're **elegance** her just 'cuz she's different."*

el·e·ment (el´-ə-mənt), *n. and v.* a clause clarifying
or summing up a past statement or action of the
speaker's. *"Sorry you thought I'd pay you back today—
element was I'd pay you back someday."*

elite (íl-ēt´), *n. and v.* a phrase predicting ingestion
by a male. *"Give it to Jake . . . **elite** anything."*

emis·sion (ə-mí´-shən), *n.* an assignment, strongly felt ambition, or calling. *"The way she's drivin' that car, she's on **emission** to fail the smog test."*

es·tate (is-stāt´), *adj. and n.* a male person's psychological status or condition. *"I wouldn't trust him in **estate** of mind."*

Eu·rope (yúr´-əp), *n. and adv.* a phrase depicting the person being spoken to as in a high or precarious position. *"I'd say **Europe** a creek without a paddle."*

eu·tha·na·sia (yü-thən-ā´-zhə), *n. and prep.* the teenage generation of the world's most populous continent. *"If the Chinese rulers get too oppressive, the **euthanasia** will rise up."*

ESTATE

EXHALED

events (i-vents´), *n. and v.* a male passionately expressing a strongly felt emotion or opinion. *"He gets mad, **events**, then he calms down."*

ev·i·dence (e´-və-dens), *v. and adj.* being in possession of something compactly heavy; or being contractually connected to a person of low intelligence. *"We coulda got off if we didn't **evidence** lawyer."*

ex·haled (eks-hāld´), *n. and v.* a former spouse having kept a thing or person in a sustained position, either literally or figuratively. *"My **exhaled** my kids over my head for more alimony."*

Ff

fac·to·ry (fakt´-ər-ē), *n. and conj.* a truth or actuality considered as a precondition of a male person's actions. *"He knew it was a **factory** wouldn't've said it."*

fad·ed (fād´-əd), *n. and v.* one's declaration of personal contempt. *"**Faded** that dude in the acid-wash jeans since I first met him."*

fair·ways (fer´-wāz), *conj. and n.* an opined conjecture concerning possible outcomes. *"**Fairways** to get in trouble, Tommy and the boys'll find them."*

fan·ta·sy (fan´-tə-sē), *n. and v.* future tense for an enthusiastic supporter perceiving visually. *"For that **fantasy** the game, you're gonna have to take your hat off."*

fart (färt), *adv. and n.* a great distance, in relation to a thing. *"My old dog will still chase a stick, but it depends how **fart** goes."*

FANTASY

FEEL

fat (fat´), *conj. and pron.* to identify, with condition or supposition. "***Fat** ain't John Goodman, it must be his twin.*"

fa·vor·ite (fā´-vər-it), *v. and n.* to give preferential treatment to a thing. "*My uncle hurt his knee in the war and now he tends to **favorite** when he walks.*"

fea·si·ble (fēz´-ə-búl), *conj. and n.* the conditional identification of an uncastrated male bovine. "***Feasible**, then I'm a cow.*"

feel (fēl´), *conj. and n.* the conditional future action of a male person or animal. "*Will you ask this kind gentleman **feel** take his hands off my throat before I die?*"

fe·line (fē´-līn), *conj. and v.* a phrase implying action conditional on the untruthfulness of a male person. *"Feline to me, I'll scratch his eyes out."*

fe·males (fē´-mālz), *conj. and v.* a phrase implying action conditional on a male person putting a package or missive into the postal system, with the purpose of its delivery to an indicated address. *"Females it today, we should have it by Friday."*

Fer·ris wheel (fer´-əs-wēl´), *adj., n., and v.* equitable treatment or judgment, as applied to a group. *"The pitcher's daddy is the umpire, so I reckon that last call is as Ferris wheel get."*

fer·tile (fər´-til), *n. and conj.* the dense, hairy coat of an animal, up to a certain point in time. *"That dog done scratched his fertile it bled."*

FERRIS WHEEL

FIZZY

fi·as·co (fē-as´-gō), *conj., n., and v.* regarding an outcome conditional on the deterioration of the buttocks. *"She looks okay now, but **fiasco**, we're through."*

fire·side (fir´-sīd), *conj. and n.* a phrase used to introduce the conditional action of a group in opposition to or competition with another. *"If your side wins, we wash your cars; **fireside** wins, you wash ours."*

fiz·zy (fiz´-ē), *prep., adj., and n.* concerning a male person and something belonging to him or intended to involve him. *"At my wedding my best man wore a tux, but **fizzy** wore his work clothes."*

fleet (flēt´), *conj. and v.* a phrase regarding the conditional future mastication of a male. *"We don't have enough food, so don't ask him **fleet** with us."*

Flor·i·da (flôr´-ə-də), *n. and prep.* a room's lower plane, upon which everything else rests, or a place where elected officials assemble for the purpose of passing laws, with reference to the larger entity. *"In three years, no new bills got passed on the **Florida** senate."*

flu·id (flü´-əd), *n. and v.* the predicted effect of a viral sickness that causes fever, chills, sneezing, and a cough. *"My gramma's so dehydrated, if she caught the **fluid** kill her."*

for·eign·er (fôr´-in-ər), *n. and prep.* an interior measurement of more than three but fewer than five persons or objects. *"Our town tried for the record for the most people in a telephone booth, but we could only get **foreigner**."*

France (frants´), *prep. and n.* with regard to insects in the family Formicidae. *"We killed all the cockroaches and termites, but we gotta check **France**."*

FOREIGNER

GASTRIC

freight (frāt´), *prep. and n.* with regard to a group of objects or units numbering twice as many as four. *"He's on a hunger strike . . . he hasn't eaten freight days."*

gar·ter (gärd´-ər), *v. and adj.* to protect or keep safe something belonging to a female. *"She eats with one arm in front of her plate to garter food."*

gas·tric (gas´-trik), *n.* a skillful act involving a flammable vaporous or liquid substance. *"Since he set his backside on fire, he don't do that gastric no more."*

Gem·i·ni (jem´-ən-ī), *n. and conj.* the speaker, as linked to a person with the given name James. *"Believe it or not, Gemini is identical twins."*

gram·mar school (gra´-mə-skül´), *n.* an educational institution for female progenitors of mothers or fathers. *"Man, there must be some kind of **grammar school** teaches them all to yell like that."*

guz·zle (gəs´-əl), *n. and v.* the predicted action of a person who goes by a nickname for Gustav. *"Dave can knock back the bourbon, but **guzzle** drink you under the table."*

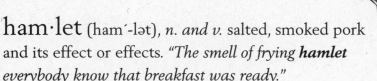

Hh

ham·let (ham´-lət), *n. and v.* salted, smoked pork and its effect or effects. *"The smell of frying **hamlet** everybody know that breakfast was ready."*

healthy (hel´-thē), *n., conj., and pron.* the eternal damnation of a male person, dependent upon certain conditions. *"He's going to **healthy** don't change his ways."*

GRAMMAR SCHOOL

HIGH-SPEED

HYSTERIA

IMPEDE

Ii

im·mi·grate (imʹ-ə-grāt), *n. and adj.* part of a phrase declaring a debt to a male. *"I owe **immigrate** deal of my success."*

im·pede (im-pēdʹ), *n. and v.* a male having urinated. *"Dangit, **impede** all over the fish I caught."*

im·plants (im-plantsʹ), *adj. and n.* more than one living multicellular organism that through photosynthesis absorbs water and carbon dioxide and emits oxygen. *"**Implants** are all saggy; they look like they could use some water."*

in·no·cence (inʹ-o-sints), *prep., n., and adv.* a phrase describing a quality of or substance within a woman after a certain circumstance. *"She married that jerk, and I ain't seen a lick of happiness **innocence**."*

in·sid·i·ous (in-sid´-ē-əs), *adv., n., and v.* an action by or quality of a male, as an alternative to another action or quality. *"We thought he was loyal, but **insidious** stabbin' us in the back."*

in·ter·est·ing (in´-tə-res-ting), *prep. and n.* having a preference for relaxation. *"Bob said he was a good pilot, but now I see he's more **interesting**."*

in·ter·view (in-tər-vyü´), *prep. and n.* entering a position that allows visual perception. *"Just shoot as soon as it comes **interview**!"*

in·un·dat·ed (in´-ən-dāt-əd), *prep. and v.* to have entered and commenced courtship. *"That snake snuck **inundated** my girl when I was out of town."*

INTERESTING

JOURNAL

iPod (ī´-päd), *n. and v.* a personal reference to having groped or roughly handled another person or an object. *"**iPod** her for about twenty minutes before I realized she was my mother-in-law."*

iron (ī´-ərn), *n. and v.* a personal proclamation about the currency one receives in exchange for the services one renders. *"Workin' down in the mine, **iron** twenty-three bucks an hour."*

J j

jour·nal (jər´-nol), *n. and v.* a proclamation excluding the person being addressed from a group. *"Don't make fun of me, Al . . . **journal** Einstein yourself!"*

ju·di·cious (jü-dish´-əs), *n. and v.* interrogative regarding whether the person being addressed spoke critically of the speaker and his or her associates. *"Sorry I called you a gossip, but didn't **judicious** a while back?"*

juic·er (jü´-sər), *pron. and n.* the start of an ironic pronouncement addressed to a male person of authority or distinction. *"I knew Jack Kennedy, and **juicer** are no Jack Kennedy."*

junc·tion (jənk´-shən), *n. and v.* a phrase assessing the state of debris in a negative way. *"That **junction** be left at the dump, stupid!"*

junk·ies (jənk´-ēz), *n. and v.* a phrase connecting useless or discarded articles to the actions of a male person. *"Don't buy any of that **junkies** sellin', 'cuz he'll only use it to buy drugs."*

Kk

Kat·man·du (kat-man´-dü), *n. and v.* a mythical character with feline qualities and his actions or function. *"I get why we let Aquaman into the club, but what the hell's the **Katmandu**?"*

KATMANDU

LAMINATE

Khar·toum (kär-tüm´), *n. and prep.* a phrase connecting an automobile with a male person. *"Paul's been actin' all high and mighty since Pa died and left the Khartoum."*

la·dle (lā´-dil), *v. and conj.* at rest or repose up to a mentioned time or event. *"Just let it ladle everybody cools off a bit."*

lam·i·nate (lam´-en-āt), *n. and v.* a young sheep, in relation to something it is not. *"I ordered the laminate cooked the way I wanted it."*

la·ser (lāz´-ər), *v. and adj.* a female's setting down of something. *"As soon as she laser big butt down for a nap, we're leaving."*

left field (left-fēld´), *n. and v.* an object located on the opposite of the right side, and the tactile sensation it elicited. *"I don't know, man, her **left field** way bigger than her right."*

less·er (les´-ər), *conj. and adj.* except if, as pertaining to a female. *"**Lesser** mom changes her mind, I don't think we're going out tonight."*

Le·vi (lēv´-ī), *v. and n.* a phrase connecting the act of departure to the speaker. *"If I **Levi** ain't coming back."*

li·ar (lī´-ər), *v. and adj.* to set or put down something of a female's. *"I don't care if she's cheating on me, she can **liar** head on my pillow anytime."*

LEFT FIELD

LUNAR

lu·nar (lün´-ər), *n. and conj.* a person afflicted with mental instability and a possible alternative. *"Is Betty a **lunar** what?"*

lu·rid (lür´-əd), *n. and v.* a conjecture about an object intended to decoy or tempt. *"I'd be shocked if that **lurid** catch fish."*

 Mm

ma·chete (mə-shed´-ē), *adj. and n.* the speaker's freestanding storage structure as acted upon by a male. *"It weren't **machete** knocked down, it was my neighbor's."*

ma·jor (mā´-jər), *v. and n.* a phrase proclaiming that the person being spoken to has been forced or induced to do something. *"Ha ha, **major** look!"*

man·i·cure (man´-ə-kyür), *n. and v.* an adult male person offered as relief for the symptoms of a disease or condition. *"If you're feeling frisky a good **manicure** you."*

ma·ple (mā´-pəl), *v. aux. and v.* expressing the possibility of the act of yanking. *"Timmy's adorable, but he **maple** your hair out."*

march (märch´), *adj. and n.* a curved structure, as of a ceiling or instep, belonging to the speaker. *"The podiatrist said my left foot is flat, so if I wanna be in the parade, I'll need better support for **march**."*

mas·och·ist (mas´-əu-kist), *n. and v.* the act of pressing one's lips against a person or object in relation to the celebration of the Christian Eucharist. *"I'm sure I'll suffer for it later, but during the first **masochist** the widow Johnson, and during the second **masochist** her sister."*

MAPLE

MAYOR

may·hem (mā´-hem), *v. aux. and v.* the possibility of, through the act of sewing, altering an article of clothing so as to shorten it or neaten its edge. *"These pants are a little long, so I **mayhem** 'em."*

may·or (mā´-yər), *v. and adj.* a term expressing a possibility associated with the person being addressed. *"Here's to you, Jenny . . . **mayor** problems be few, now that your mother, that witch, is dead and gone!"*

mean (mēn), *pron. and conj.* the speaker plus some- one related to a female. *"**Mean** her sister wandered off behind the barn for a while."*

men·stru·ate (men´-strāt), *n. and adj.* adult males gaining through understanding. *"About once a month my wife acts like she's got to set all **menstruate** about somethin'."*

men·tion (men´-shən), *n. and v.* the start of a proclamation expressing a desired restriction on male behavior. "***Mention*** *wear skirts, unless they're Scottish.*"

menu (men´-yü), *n. and pron.* adult human males in relation to the person being addressed. "*Wolfgang Puck is one of the richest **menu** would ever want to meet.*"

min·i·a·ture (min´-ə-chùr), *n., prep., and adj.* more than one adult male person in a particular position or relation to the person being addressed. "*I thought you said there was gonna be a lot of hot **miniature** party.*"

min·is·ter (min´-ə-stər), *n. and v.* the speaker's avowal to personally create agitation. "*If that preacher shows up here tonight, **minister** up a whole lot of trouble.*"

MINIATURE

MIXTURE

mi·sog·y·ny (mə-säj´-en-ē), *n. and conj.* the act of kneading muscles in order to relieve tension, as linked to a male. *"He was gettin' a **misogyny** fell asleep halfway through."*

mix·ture (miks´-chər), *v. and adj.* to have combined or melded two or more substances, at least one of them belonging to the person being addressed. *"You **mixture** chocolate in my peanut butter."*

mon·key (mən´-kē), *adj. and n.* the speaker's ownership of an instrument that provides access to a locked place. *"I can go to the zoo whenever I like—I got **monkey**."*

mon·soon (män´-sün), *n., v., and adv.* the speaker's proclamation that in a short period of time he or she will be expected to proceed to a stage, usually to perform entertainment. *"I'm sure you could give me a few pointers on my jokes, dude, but I don't have the time, 'cuz **monsoon**."*

mor·al (mȯr´-əl), *adv. and conj.* to a greater extent, with the possibility of an alternative. *"I've been to that strip club a hundred times, **moral** less."*

mor·bid (mȯr´-bid), *adj. and n.* another offer. *"One **morbid** like that and this auction's closed!"*

Mos·cow (mäs´-kaù), *adj. and n.* a female bovine owned by the speaker's female parent. *"Dad's new wife is gonna have a fit if we don't get **Moscow** outta his barn."*

mov·ies (müv´-ēz), *v. and n.* a phrase connecting a male to a change of position. *"If he doesn't **movies** in big trouble."*

MOVIES

NOODLE

mum·mi·fy (məm´-if-ī), *n. and conj.* a conditional phrase connecting the speaker to the female
who gave birth to him or her. *"I'll hafta ask my
mummify can play with that weird Egyptian kid."*

 Nn

na·sal (nāz´-əl), *n. and v.* a phrase used to express an
opinion or observation about a group as a whole. *"See
them guys? **Nasal** a bunch of jerks."*

net·works (net´-wərkz), *n. and v.* the functioning
of a woven trap. *"We'll catch a lot of fish if this
networks."*

noo·dle (nü´-dəl), *adj. and conj.* in pristine condition, and the termination of that status. *"My truck was
brand-**noodle** I drove it into that tree."*

nurse·maid (nərs´-mād), *n. and v.* caused by a caregiver to the ill. *"She's so hot, that **nursemaid** my blood pressure go up."*

of·fice (äf´-fəs), *prep. and adj.* a phrase stating that a male no longer occupies or is in possession of something that belongs to him. *"If he thinks I'm working on Superbowl Sunday, he's **office** rocker."*

Ophe·lia (ə-fēl´-yə), *n. and v.* used to declare empathy for another's physical or spiritual discomfort. *"**Ophelia** pain."*

or·ange (är´-inj), *v. and adv.* a contraction of "are not"; usually used as an interrogative. *"**Orange** you glad I didn't drive drunk?"*

NURSEMAID

ORDEAL

or·deal (ȯr-dēl´), *conj. and v.* a phrase connecting something to an alternative involving the act of distribution. *"Quit the game **ordeal** the cards!"*

ori·ga·mi (ȯr-ə-gä´-mē), *conj. and v.* a phrase connecting something to an alternative involving something possessed by the speaker. *"I could use this, **origami** a twelve-gauge in the cab."*

ox·en (äks´-ən), *n. and prep.* a domesticated bovine, encased or enclosed. *"If we put that boy Bos taurus with that girl Bos taurus, pretty soon we'll have a baby **oxen** here."*

pal·ace (pal´-əs), *n. and conj.* an ally compared to something else. *"The king is not as good a **palace** you think he is."*

pan·da (pan´-də), *n. and prep.* a metal container used for cooking, as connected to an action. *"That ain't the **panda** asked for, stupid!"*

para·chute (per´-ə-shüt), *n. and v.* two human beings and the prediction that they will cause a pro-jectile to move at a high velocity. *"Watch out for Bonnie and Clyde, 'cuz that **parachute** ya just for fun."*

par·a·mount (per´-ə-maunt), *n. and v.* two living beings and the prediction that they will climb atop. *"The most important thing to know about rabbits is that they're so frisky, a **paramount** one female."*

para·noia (per´-ə-noi-ə), *n. and v.* two living be-ings engaging in irritating behavior. *"You can't let that **paranoia**."*

PARANOIA

PARODY

par·o·dy (per´-ə-dē), *n. and pron.* a phrase connecting two matched things or a single thing composed of two matched parts to a male. *"He wanted a pair of pants, but them ain't the **parody** wanted."*

par·ty (pärt´-ē), *n. and pron.* a phrase connecting one segment of a whole, as with a character in a performance, to a male. *"He was only wearing a dress 'cuz that was the **party** was tryin' out for."*

pas·tor (past´-ər), *adj. and conj.* a phrase connecting a time gone by to an alternative. *"All my wives, **pastor** present, have been preachers' daughters."*

pen·i·cil·lin (pen-ə-sil´-ən), *n. and v.* a writing or drawing instrument that uses ink being offered in exchange for currency. *"I think it's sick that this **penicillin** for two grand!"*

phrase (frāz´), *prep. and n.* with regard to an increase in salary. *"Will you ask your boss **phrase**?"*

pi·ous (pī´-əs), *n. and v.* a declarative phrase concerning the state of a baked meat or fruit dish with a crusted pastry top. *"This **pious** so good, God musta made it hisself!"*

prais·es (prāz´-əz), *v. and adj.* a male person performing an act of solemn communion with a deity, as connected to something belonging to that male. *"My grandaddy **praises** knees off."*

pres·sure (pre´-shər), *v. and adj.* to apply continual force to something belonging to the one being addressed. *"Just pull out the dart and **pressure** hands down on the wound so we can finish the game."*

PRESSURE

QUARTER

pri·ma·ry (prī´-mer-ē), *v. and n.* to exert force on, with the purpose of pulling off or apart, a person with the same name as the mother of Jesus. *"She was so mad, it took four grown men to **primary** off her first husband."*

quar·ter (kort´-ər), *n. and adj.* a legal tribunal and its effect on or relation to a female person. *"Not only was she drunk, but when she got to **quarter** lawyer was drunk too."*

ra·zor (rāz´-ər), *n. and conj.* an alternative to an increase in salary or wages. *"I told my boss, 'Either you give me a **razor** I quit!' "*

reck·on (rek´-ən), *v.* the ongoing act of destroying or demolishing. *"I keep buying 'em, she keeps **reckon** 'em."*

rig·id (rij´-əd), *n. and v.* a narrow hilltop and conjecture or suggested possibilities concerning it. *"That **rigid** be hard to climb without a pair of stiff-soled boots."*

rit·u·al (rich´-ü-əl), *adj. and v.* a phrase predicting the actions of a person in the presence of great financial means. *"I know if you ever get **ritual** buy a yacht the first day."*

Ro·man (rōm´-ən), *v.* to be in the midst of wandering. *"That crazy lady been **Roman** around the coliseum for hours."*

RECKON

SANDWICH

rug·ged (rəg´-əd), *n. and v.* a woven floor mat or a toupee and conjecture or suggested possibilities for it. *"That **rugged** look better if you cleaned it once in a while."*

Ss

sad·ist (saʸd´-ist), *adj.* the highest degree of sorrow or unhappiness. *"It makes me sad when somebody hurts me, but it makes me **sadist** when I hurt somebody else."*

sand·wich (sand´-wich), *n. and pron.* granular soil, usually composed of eroded siliceous rock and commonly found near water, considered in relation to a person or thing. *"My bathing suit was full of **sandwich** made my butt itch."*

Sa·rah (ser´-ə), *v. and adv.* interrogative concerning the location or existence of a thing. *"Hey, baby, **Sarah** another beer in the fridge?"*

scep·ter (sep´-tər), *prep. and adj.* other than something of a female's. *"She came out of the house wearing nothing scepter bra and panties."*

schol·ar (skälh´-ər), *v. and n.* a phrase in which the speaker suggests, to one or more others, telephonic communication with a female. *"Scholar after we've had a few more drinks."*

scrab·ble (skrab´-əl), *n. and v.* a specific crustacean of the order Decapoda and possibilities for it. *"Scrabble taste real good . . . all we have to do is kill it."*

sea·food (sē´-füd), *v. and n.* to perceive, through the ocular organs, nutritious substances. *"My problem is whenever I seafood, I eat food."*

SCRABBLE

SINCERE

sei·zure (sē´-zhər), *v. and adj.* to match another's bet when gaming or gambling. *"I believe you're bluffin', so I **seizure** nickel and raise you ten grand."*

sew·er (sü´-ər), *v. and n.* to take legal action against a female, usually with the purpose of financial redress. *"If she don't give me my money, I'm gonna **sewer** for everything she's got!"*

Sher·wood (shər´-wŭd), *adv. and v.* an intensive phrase suggesting the certainty of an imagined action. *"It **Sherwood** help if I could get a job with the Forest Service."*

sin·cere (sins´-ir), *v. and adv.* to blaspheme in a particular place. *"If he **sincere** in church, he's in deep trouble."*

Sod·om and Go·mor·rah (sä´-dəm-ənd-gə-
mȯr´-ə), *v., n., conj., v., and n.* a phrase describing the
ocular perception of more than one thing, plus the re-
sulting action of acquiring additional amounts of those
things. *"I didn't have enough doughnuts for my orgy, so
when I went to the bakery I **Sodom and Gomorrah** the
honey-glazed."*

sol·emn (säl´-əm), *n. and pron.* a phrase declaring
the limit or tally of a number of things or people. *"I
expected a bigger turnout at Ken's funeral, but **solemn**."*

so·lo (sō´-lō), *adv. and adj.* dishonest or morally re-
pugnant, to a certain extent. *"How could you stoop **solo**
as to date my mother?"*

soph·ist·ry (säf´-əs-trē), *adj. and n.* an arborescent
plant having the smoothest and most pleasing quality
to the touch. *"This is the **sophistry** I ever felt."*

SOPHISTRY

SPAIN

Spain (spān´), *adj. and n.* a specific sharp physical or emotional discomfort. *"I'm going to the doctor. **Spain** in my leg won't go away."*

speed (spēd´), *n. and v.* the past tense of a male performing the function of urination. *"He's so drunk, he don't even know **speed** his pants."*

spir·it (spir´-ət), *v. and n.* to stab a creature or an inanimate object with a sharpened staff. *"I ran out of shells, so I hadda **spirit**."*

stew·ard (stə´-wərd), *v. and n.* a phrase pertaining to specific information or news. *"Hey, what'**steward** on the street?"*

sto·ries (stȯr´-ēz), *n., pron., and v.* a phrase connecting a retail establishment to a male. *"Every time he comes into this **stories** drunk."*

stride (strīd´), *n. and v.* having made attempts in the past. *"He says he can quit smokin' anytime, but **stride** and failed a hundred times."*

study (stəd´-ē), *n. and pron.* a virile or sexually active specimen or type in relation to another male. *"He's not half the **study** thinks he is."*

sum·mit (səm´-ət), *v. and n.* to review a number of thoughts or themes and synthesize them into a single, unifying concept. *"Well, to **summit** all up, Stan's an idiot."*

STRIDE

SYCAMORE

sump·tu·ous (səm´-shəs), *n. and adv.* a subset of a group, simply. *"Most folks think he's cool, but **sumptuous** think he's a jerk."*

Su·per Bowl (süp´-pər-bōl), *n., prep., and n.* a simmered food in liquid stock in relation to each shallow, concave container in which it is served. *"It's only supposed to be one servin' of **Super Bowl**."*

syc·a·more (sik´-ə-mȯr), *v. and adv.* to direct an attack with something grander than the original. *"To scare those bad guys you're gonna need to **sycamore** frightening dog on 'em."*

syn·di·cate (sin´-də-kit), *v., prep., and n.* indicating the location of a thing as enclosed within a container. *"He asked me where my shaving things are, and I told him they'**syndicate**."*

tat·too (ta-tü´), *prep. and n.* up to a couple of hours past midday or midnight. *"I can only stay **tattoo**—then I gotta get back to work."*

tele·phone (tel´-ə-fōn), *v. and n.* to recognize or perceive a fact concerning a device that converts acoustic vibrations to a transmittable electronic signal. *"You can **telephone** never rang, 'cuz there's no incoming calls displayed."*

ten·der·ize (ten´-dər-īz), *adj. and n.* ocular organs that exude qualities of sympathy and gentleness. *"Her face was mean, but she had **tenderize**."*

Ten·nes·see (ten´-ə-sē), *n. and v.* wherein the speaker expresses that he or she visually perceives a thing or person that would earn the highest rating in a decimal system. *"Ben said everyone here's from Nashville, but you're the only **Tennessee**."*

TATTOO

THERAPY

ten·u·ous (ten´-yü-əs), *n. and v.* a person's state of being during a past period of life when their age in years, counting from moment of birth, fell between nine and eleven. *"When you was **tenuous** eighty pounds—how in the world did you double that in a year and a half?!"*

ther·a·py (ther´-ə-pē), *adv. and n.* a phrase connecting urination to a particular time or place. *"Is **therapy** break anytime soon?"*

this·tle (this´-əl), *n. and v.* a prediction about a specific thing or event. *"**Thistle** be easy!"*

tis·sue (tish´-ü), *adv. and n.* a phrase wherein the speaker declares the singularity of the person being spoken to. *"**Tissue** and me tonight, baby."*

ti·tan (tīt´-ən), *v.* to make more secure. *"Them giant pants wouldn't fall down if you'd **titan** your belt up."*

touch·stone (təch´-stōn), *v. and prep.* to have broached. *"You've done **touchstone** a sensitive subject."*

tra·peze (trap´-ēz), *n. and v.* a device for snaring or capturing prey, connected to a male. *"If he misses the first **trapeze** gonna fall in the second one for sure."*

tri·ple (trip´-əl), *n. and v.* a journey and its pre-dicted result. *"If you think Three Mile Island is a nice vacation spot, one **triple** change your mind."*

TOUCHSTONE

TUNNEL

tuck·er (tək´-ər), *v. and adj.* to neaten, by pulling something in or by placing one piece of clothing inside another, something of a female's. *"Tell her to **tucker** butt back into her shorts."*

tun·nel (tən´-əl), *n. and v.* a prediction concerning something that weighs two thousand pounds. *"When the waiter asked my wife how much chocolate sauce she wanted on her ice cream, I said a **tunnel** do."*

turn (tərn´), *v.* to obtain deservedly. *"You need to get the basketball through the hoop **turn** points."*

tu·tor (tü´-tər), *n. and prep.* the consequence or effect of a pair of things. *"One drink just gets her flirty . . . it takes **tutor** get the clothes off."*

twine (twīn), *n.* an alcoholic beverage made from fermented grapes. *"'Twas **twine** talkin'."*

Uu

un·canny (ən-kan´-ē), *prep. and v.* interrogative connecting the abilities of a male to a position over or on top of a particular location. *"It's really weird, but he can't get **uncanny**?"*

unit (yü´-nit), *n. and v.* a phrase connecting the one being addressed to the act of creating a garment or other piece of fabric by using yarn and needles. *"Gramma, will **unit** me a sweater?"*

uri·nal (yər´-ən-əl), *n. and v.* a declaration concerning the current status or location of the person being spoken to. *"If you think **urinal** lot of trouble now, just wait till Daddy gets home."*

URINAL

VALID

val·id (val´-əd), *n. and v.* the predicted action of a person named Valentine, Valentino, Valdemar, Valdez, or Valenzuela. "*Valid go out with a monkey if you put a dress on it.*"

val·i·date (val´-əd-dāt), *n. and v.* the predicted courtship or social engagement of a person named Valentine, Valentino, Valdemar, Valdez, or Valenzuela. "*He's so desperate since that monkey dumped him, now validate anything that moves!*"

Val·ium (va´-lē-əm), *n. and v.* a low area between hills, in relation to the speaker. "*I'm too tired to go any farther, so this is the last Valium walking through.*"

vir·gin (vər´-jən), *v.* to be approaching or coming close to. "*She's so loose, she's virgin on bein' a tramp.*"

vi·sor (vīz´-ər), *conj., n., and v.* the start of a speaker's opinion about a particular female. *"Visor, I'd lose the baseball cap."*

vi·ta·min (vīt´-əm-ən), *v. and n.* to formally request the presence of a male in an enclosed structure or at a gathering. *"He's your friend, so if you want him at the party, you vitamin."*

vix·en (vik´-sən), *v.* preparing. *"We're vixen to eat dinner."*

wait·er (wāt´-ər), *v. and conj.* a phrase linking staying in one's current location or delaying action to an alternative. *"I think we'd better waiter we're going to be sorry."*

WAITER

WINERIES

ware·hous·es (wer´-haús-ez), *adv. and n.* a phrase connecting a place to structures for habitation. *"Since the tornado hit, there's just dirt **warehouses** used to be."*

wary (wer´-ē), *adv. and n.* a phrase connecting a place to a male. *"I might be able to get my money back if I knew **wary** lived."*

whit·en·er (wī´-tin-ər), *adv. and v.* interrogative regarding the past actions of someone or something of a female's. *"If she was sick, **whitener** mother call the school and let them know?"*

win·eries (wīn´-ər-ēz), *n. and conj.* a phrase linking an alcoholic beverage made from fermented grapes to alternative actions of a male person. *"Just get him another glass of **wineries** gonna start making a scene."*

win·ner (win´-ər), *adv. and adj.* with temporal regard to someone or something connected to a female. *"Tell me **winner** car pulls into the driveway."*

wor·ri·some (wər´-ē-səm), *v. and n.* a subjunctive phrase regarding a male's state or condition. *"I'd have been anxious **worrisome** sort of jerk."*

Xx

xy·lene (zī´-lēn), *n. and v.* to incline one's body. *"He hurt me with his left hook, 'cuz **xylene** to the right."*

Yy

ya·hoo (yä-hü´), *interj. and pron.* interrogative regarding which person or persons. *"Shut up?! **Yahoo** is gonna come over here and make me?!"*

WINNER

ZIT

yearn (yərnˊ), *n. and v.* interrogative concerning the financial compensation a person obtained in exchange for labor. *"**Yearn** anything last year?"*

You·Tube (yü´-tüb), *adj. and n.* a stretchy cylindrical article of clothing belonging to the person being addressed. *"Put on **YouTube** top, baby, we're goin' out someplace nice tonight!"*

Zz

ze·roed (zē´-rōd), *n. and v.* a male who has just traveled, as on the back of an animal. *"Screw him and the horse **zeroed** on."*

zit (zitˊ), *v. and n.* interrogative regarding the effect of a specific thing. *"Mama, this pimple on my forehead—**zit** gonna ruin my date?"*

ABOUT THE AUTHOR

JEFF FOXWORTHY is the largest-selling comedy-recording artist in history, a multiple Grammy Award nominee, and the bestselling author of more than twenty books. He is the host of the Fox television series *Are You Smarter Than a 5th Grader?* Prior to that he was the star and executive producer of the CMT series *Foxworthy's Big Night Out*, and he starred in and executive-produced the series *Blue Collar TV*, which he also created. Jeff also starred in all three *Blue Collar Comedy Tour* movies, which have sold more than 8 million copies and are some of the highest-rated movies in Comedy Central history. His syndicated weekly radio show, *The Foxworthy Countdown*, is carried in more than 220 markets across the United States.

Offstage and -screen, Jeff has helped the Duke University Children's Hospital raise millions of dollars and is the honorary chairman of the Duke Children's Classic Golf Tournament. A Georgia native, he lives with his wife and two daughters in Atlanta.

ABOUT THE TYPE

This book was set in Berling. Designed in 1951 by Karl Erik Forsberg for the Typefoundry Berlingska Stilgjuteri AB in Lund, Sweden, it was released the same year in foundry type by H. Berthold AG. A classic old-face design, its generous proportions and inclined serifs make it highly legible.